Every day is a gift

daily devotions

Erin Lyn Burks

ISBN-13: 978-1517403218
ISBN-10: 1517403219

CreateSpace Independent Publishing Platform, North Charleston, SC

Cherish and embrace this wonderful life you have been
blessed with, every second, every moment......
every day is a gift!

Gift

Every single day is a gift you should cherish. Make time to enjoy the simple things in life that God has blessed you with. We are not promised tomorrow, so live life today!

Yesterday is history; tomorrow is unknown; today is a gift, that is why it is called the present.

"Every good and perfect gift is from above, coming down from the Father of the heavenly lights." - James 1:17

Did you open your gift today?

Five

Life is busy. We have this never-ending 'to do' list running through our head. Do you feel like your daily list is full and there isn't room for one more single thing?

How can we fit prayer time and quiet time with God into our hectic daily lives? We need to find time to talk with Him and listen for his guidance

Make five minutes. If we give Him our time, God can do more within us in five minutes than we can all day on our own. Jesus came that we may have a full life, but I am pretty sure he didn't mean a full 'to do' list.

"And whatever you do, whether in word or deed, do it all in the name of the Lord Jesus, giving thanks to God the Father through him." – Colossians 3:17

Can you make 5 minutes?

Rewritten

We should not try to change the scriptures in the bible to make them agree with the way we choose to live our life. The Gospel is meant to change the sinner, not for the sinner to change the Gospel to suit their sin.

The Bible can't be like a bag of trail mix, picking out the pieces you like and ignoring the rest.

Don't let your circumstances change your view of God. Let God change your view of the circumstances.

"Scripture cannot be broken." – John 10:35

Have you tried to rewrite the bible?

Believe

Do you believe in God? The answer seems pretty simple, 'Yes! I believe!'

What are you actually going to do about it? We can't just say we believe in God, even the devil believes in God. We need to LIVE for God.

At Calvary Jesus rearranged the letters of EVIL to now read - LIVE.

"If you confess with your mouth," Jesus is Lord," and believe in your heart that God raised him from the dead, you will be saved." - Romans 10:9

Are you living for God?

Good

There is good in the world – even if that belief is challenged on a daily basis. If we can change our thoughts we can change the world.

We need more kindness and less judgment and negativity in the world. Be the light for others. Do all things with kindness.

BE THE GOOD!!

"Therefore encourage one another and build each other up." – 1 Thessalonians 5:11

Whose life can you impact today?

Blesson

Life may not be going the way we planned, but through faith we know our life is going exactly the way God planned it.

A 'blesson' happens when you are able to see the blessing in the lesson you had to go through.

Life is all about perspective. The happiness of your life depends on the quality of your thoughts.

"For I know the plans I have for you," declares the Lord, "plans to proposer you and not to harm you, plans to give you hope and a future." - Jeremiah 29:11

Are you having a blesson day?

Door

Open the door of your heart to Christ. He stands outside, waiting for us to invite Him in. If you believe that Christ was born to be your Savior, and that he died for your sins, open the door, invite Christ in.

When that door is opened, something wonderful happens; Christ, the light of the world, will come in.

"Here I am! I stand at the door and knock. If anyone hears my voice and opens the door, I will come in." - Revelation 3:20

Is your door opened?

Trust

If you learn and understand things easier when you can see or visualize them, it may be a struggle to believe without seeing first.

We have to remember that God loves us unconditionally, so we must also believe unconditionally. Trust God, even when we can't see his plan.

Let God's perfect peace surround you as you trust in Him in all things.

"We live by faith, not by sight."
– 2 Corinthians 5:7

Do you trust God unconditionally?

Me

When life isn't going the way we planned, we start to question, 'Is God for me?' We can feel alone and wonder if He realizes and even cares what we are going through.

God hasn't left us, he is right here, right now, always and forever. When we feel alone, we need to realize we are the ones that have walked away. God will never leave us and he will never forsake us.

We are where God wants us to be at this very moment, every experience is part of his divine plan.

"If God is for us, who can be against us?"
– Romans 8:31

Maybe we need to ask ourselves the question..........

Are we for God?

Problems

When we have problems in life, we might share them with friends, family, or even on social media. Do you share them with God?

God won't always offer you immediate solutions, or make all your problems disappear. But if you place your faith and trust in Him and confide in God, he will enable you to think clearly, giving you guidance and wisdom.

He will give you the strength to handle your problems according to His will.

"Cast all your anxiety on him because he cares for you." – 1 Peter 5:7

Who do you share your problems with?

Privileged

Serving God and worshiping Him are not simply duties we have to perform but actually awesome privileges.

Enjoy your life with Christ. Allow Him to become part of your daily life, then you will discover the fullness of life that He offers you.

Think of what a valuable privilege it is to be alive, to breathe, to think, to enjoy, to love.

"Praise the Lord. Give thanks to the Lord, for he is good; his love endures forever."
– Psalm 106:1

Are you privileged?

Envy

We may envy people because they have things that we want. We forget that material things do not determine our joy. Only a healthy relationship with God can ensure that we will have eternal, everlasting joy.

Praise God for the blessings that He gives you. Give Him thanks for His goodness and abundant grace.

We don't need more to be thankful for, we just need to be more thankful.

"Give thanks to the Lord, for he is good. His love endures forever." - Psalm 136:1

Are you envious of others?

Tape

Negativity is all around us; the newspaper, gossip at the coffee shop, drama on social media. Negative words seem to come out of our mouth easier.

I wonder why God doesn't put duct tape on our mouths? The devil loves to hear negative talk, to see pain and suffering all around us.

A positive world can be all around us too, but we might have to look harder for those events, work harder to speak those words. The devil tries to put duct tape over our mouth to silence us when we want to praise God.

"Do not let any unwholesome talk come out of your mouths, but only what is helpful for building others up according to their needs, that it may benefit those who listen."
-Ephesians 4:29

Are you speaking positive words?

Afraid

Fear can be caused when we think our needs or the needs of someone we love will be taken away or not met.

We might be afraid we are going to have to face something we don't understand, and face it alone.

God's Word promises that He will never forsake you. He will never abandon you. He will not give up on you.

"I sought the Lord, and he answered me; he delivered me from all my fears." – Psalm 34:4

What are you afraid of?

Gear

Each morning when you wake up, you get to decide what type of day you are going to have. Don't start the day in neutral, waiting for someone or something to dictate your day.

Instead, before you even get out of bed each morning, decide, 'Today is a good day for a good day!'

Life is all about perspective. Be thankful for what you do have. Say to yourself, 'I'm too blessed to complain.' A smile on your face doesn't mean that your life is perfect, it means you appreciate what God has blessed you with.

"Give thanks in all circumstances, for this is God's will for you in Christ Jesus."
– 1 Thessalonians 5:18

What gear are you in?

Label

Don't let others label you, dictating who you are and what your future holds.

Only God and you get to decide what label to wear. Be the person God created you to be - You!

We need to love more and label less.

"Before I formed you in the womb I knew you, before you were born I set you apart."
- Jeremiah 1:5

Do you label others?

Morning

When you get up in the morning, find something to be thankful for. It could be something really big, or simple and small.

Some days it may be harder to see your blessings. On those days, slow down and really look around, see what God has given you to enjoy. You can always find something if you rise and shine and give God the glory!

To have a good morning – be thankful for God's morning.

"Let the morning bring me word of your unfailing love." - Psalm 143:8

Are you having a God's morning?

Partner

God wants a partnership with us. Talk with Him, open your heart to God. Tell him exactly what is bothering you or what you need guidance and clarity with.

He may not answer you the way you wanted and he may not answer you right away, but he will hear you.

Jesus didn't come to start a religion, he came to form a relationship with you. He wants your will and His will to blend together, to form an amazing union.

"For God so loved the world that he gave his one and only Son, that whoever believes in him shall not perish but have eternal life."
- John 3:16

Is God your partner?

Blessed

Sometimes our struggles seem worse at night. When sunrise comes and we are blessed with a new day, it brings hope again that we can continue.

Every day has a new beginning, so take a deep breath and start again. Don't allow yourself to wake up with yesterday's issues troubling your mind.

Refuse to live backwards, but instead see everyday as a new chapter. Each new day gives us new reasons to praise the Lord.

"Weeping may remain for a night, but rejoicing comes in the morning." - Psalm 30:5

Have you been blessed with another day?

Judge

Before you judge someone else, ask yourself, 'Am I perfect?' Stop and think about all the things God has forgiven you for.

Don't judge someone else's choices since we don't know their whole story. We have no idea what storm God has asked them to walk through.

"The Lord does not look at the things man looks at. Man looks at the outward appearance, but the Lord looks at the heart."
- 1 Samuel 16:7

Do you judge?

Reputation

A reputation is fragile; once it is damaged, it's hard to restore. Are you willing to sacrifice a good reputation for power, fame, and/or profit?

God tells us that true value must be placed not in what we have, but in who we are.

"A good name is more desirable than great riches; to be esteemed is better than silver or gold." - Proverbs 22:1

God is always beside us, hearing us and watching us.

Do you make Him proud?

Abandoned

When you are experiencing a problem or have a situation, you might find yourself questioning if God abandoned you when you needed him the most.

With faith you can overcome those feelings and know that isn't true, God will never leave you! We might choose to leave God and walk away from our faith in hard times, but God will never leave us.

Remember that God has a plan for your life. It may not be an easy path, but he will be right beside you, guiding you.

"Never will I leave you; never will I forsake you." - Hebrews 13:5

Did you walk away from God?

Temporary

Our current life is temporary, but the God we worship and serve is eternal. He shared eternity with us through the gift of His Son, Jesus Christk.

God promises us a life that will never pass away. When Christ returns, He will take us home to be with Him forever!

"So we fix our eyes not on what is seen, but on what is unseen. For what is seen is temporary, but what is unseen is eternal."
– 2 Corinthians 4:18

Life on earth is short; Heaven is forever.

Is your life temporary?

Forecast

We get to control the weather in our life. Do you feel sunny today - life is going great, without a lot of problems or do you feel cloudy - life is full of struggles?

Whatever your weather forecast is for today, remember you get to control your own weather.

Don't let the sun go down, don't end your day until you have found a way to make each and every day sunny. Some days you may have to create your own sunshine.

"God is light; in him there is no darkness at all." - 1 John 1:5

What is your weather forecast?

Special

Do you have china in your cupboard that is only used for special meals? Do you have a favorite outfit you have saved for a special date?

Don't save something for a special event because every day of your life is a special occasion that should be celebrated.

Today is special!!

"I have come that they may have life, and have it to the full." – John 10:10

What are you celebrating today?

Hands

When things aren't going right, our first instinct is to try and control it. Instead God tells us, 'Hands off!' God wants to deal with your problems.

We need to trust in His wise and timely involvement in our life, keeping our hands out of His way. When we put our problems in God's hands, he puts His peace in our hearts.

It is hard to know when to take our hands off and let God work, it can definitely make us feel vulnerable unless we believe that God is indeed........

"our refuge and strength, an ever-present help in trouble." - Psalm 46:1

Do you need God's hands?

Forgive

It can be hard to forgive someone when you feel justice needs to be done. God reminds us that he is the one and only true judge, he will take care of the judging. No one has a clearer sense of right and wrong than God. Only He knows perfect justice.

We each have the opportunity to choose forgiveness for those that have done us wrong. When we forgive, it prevents their behavior from destroying our heart.

Instead of focusing on the mistakes made against us, we need to remember that none of us are perfect. God forgives our wrong doings, so we need to do the same to others.

"Be kind and compassionate to one another, forgiving each other, just as in Christ God forgave you." – Ephesians 4:32

Who do you need to forgive?

Wait

'Wait' is a word we don't like to hear. The Bible tells us that God wants us to wait for Him – for His time, not our time. Waiting on God means patiently looking to Him for what we need.

Our prayers often revolve around asking God to hurry up and bless what we want to do. What if God's answer to us is simply, 'be patient, wait on Me'?

With every prayer request that you bring to God, ensure your request also includes, 'If it is Your Will!' We can trust His response, even it if doesn't come in the time we expect. His Will. His Time.

"Be still before the Lord and wait patiently for him." - Psalm 37:7

Is it God's time or your time?

Giant

The bible tells the story of David and Goliath. Goliath, a giant with that looks invincible with his armor and David, a shepherd with only his five stones and a sling shot.

David has a weapon that Goliath doesn't though - God! David has confidence not in what he has but in who is with him.

What 'Goliath' are you facing right now? With God all things are small in comparison. Nothing is too big for Him!

Don't tell God how big your giants are, tell your giants how big your God is. God will deliver you from the 'giant' in your life, but He may do so in ways you don't expect nor planned for.

"The Lord...will deliver me." – 1 Samuel 17:37

Do you have a giant in your life?

Letters

Receiving a hand written letter in the mail is priceless, especially from a loved one. Our heavenly Father has written us many letters, all we have to do is open our bibles.

The bible provides us with so many letters of teaching and guidance, giving us power and wisdom. Every day you have the opportunity to receive a written letter from a loved one – God. Open your bible and spend time reading these scriptures.

"All Scripture is God-breathed and is useful for teaching, rebuking, correcting and training in righteousness, so that the man of God may be thoroughly equipped for every good work."
– 2 Timothy 3:16-17

Who will you send a hand written letter to?

Worry

Do you feel like you are living stressed and worried? Stress less, smile more. Worrying does not empty tomorrow of our troubles, it just drains today of our strengths.

When we have peace in our heart and mind, we draw peace into our lives.

Pray more - Worry less!

Stop focusing on how stressed you are and start focusing on how blessed you are.

"Therefore do not worry about tomorrow, for tomorrow will worry about itself."
– Matthew 6:34

Do you have peace?

Success

Most of us want to achieve success in life, but what really is success? That definition can be different for each of us.

Being successful might not be about what you have achieved, but what you have overcome.

We need Jesus Christ's guidance and support to help us make the right decisions, to stay on course and achieve success in all that we have been called to do.

"Commit to the Lord whatever you do, and your plans will succeed." - Proverbs 16:3

Do you feel successful?

Fly

When God pushes you to the edge of difficulty, trust Him completely. Because two things can happen, either He'll catch you when you fall, or He will teach you how to fly.

We may say to God, 'Show me and I'll trust you.' God turns that request around and says, 'Trust me and I'll show you.' Faith is trusting God when you don't understand his plan.

The bible never says, 'figure it out,' it says, 'trust God.'

"I can do everything through him who gives me strength." - Philippians 4:13

Will you fall or fly?

Words

Words can be used for either positive or negative results. They can build a person up or tear them down. Try to use your words for good rather than evil.

Do you speak words that have value? Always speak words that are worthy and that bring glory and honor to God.

"Do not let unwholesome talk come out of your mouth, but only what is helpful for building others up according to their needs, that it may benefit those who listen."
- Ephesians 4:29

How valuable are your words?

Resentment

Do you have resentment towards someone or something that has happened in your life? Life can make you bitter or better, you get to choose.

Ask God to help you overcome the bitterness in a situation that you can't change. Let it go!

You can't reverse what has happened, but through God's strength you can move on.

"Therefore, as God's chosen people, holy and dearly loved, clothe yourselves with compassion, kindness, humility, gentleness and patience." - Colossians 3:12

Do you choose bitter or better?

Date

God loves when you invite him on a special date. He cherishes the one-on-one quiet time with you.

If you don't think you 'have' time for a date, 'make' time. Select a time in your schedule and claim it for God. Your date with God should last long enough for you to share what is on your heart and listen to what God is saying to you.

Bring an open bible on your date. God's word is like love letters that he has written you.

"It always protects, always trusts, always hopes, always perseveres. Love never fails."
- 1 Corinthians 13:7-8

When was your last date with God?

Appreciate

Take pride in what God has blessed you with. He won't give you more until you appreciate what you have.

Don't let the things you want make you forget the things you already have. Try to start each day with a thankful heart.

"I will sing to the Lord, for he has been good to me." - Psalm 13:6

Are you appreciative?

Fear

'Do not fear' is one of most common advices found in the bible. God doesn't given you a spirit of fear. If you're feeling afraid, that's not from God, that's from the Devil.

Don't accept it - Don't give in to it. What God has given you is a spirit of power, of love, and a sound mind.

Start seeking God and don't stop. When you are always seeking God, your fears will go away.

"Do no fear, for I am with you; do not be dismayed, for I am your God. I will strengthen you and help you; I will uphold you with my righteous right hand." - Isaiah 41:10

What are you afraid of?

Pray

There isn't a right or wrong way to pray, it isn't about how the prayer is said – it is about who is hearing the prayer – God!

Prayer is a heartfelt conversation between us and God, just talk to Him. If you don't know where to start, 'The Lord's Prayer' is a great guide.

"Our Father in heaven,
hallowed be your name,
your kingdom come,
your will be done
on earth as it is in heaven.............."
        -Matthew 6:9-15

How do you pray?

Consequences

You are free to choose how you live your life, but you are not free from the consequences of your choices.

Remember that your actions affect other people. Be careful what you say and do, it's not always just about you.

"He who digs a hole and scoops it out falls into the pit he has made. The trouble he causes recoils on himself; his violence comes down on his own head." - Psalm 7:15-16

What are your consequences?

Ripples

Life is like a ripple of water. Every tidal wave begins with just a ripple.

Make sure the ripples you create in your life are what you want coming back to you; because eventually, they will return.

When you are living the best version of yourself, you inspire others to live the best version of themselves.

"In everything set them an example by doing what is good." - Titus 2:7

What type of ripples do you make?

Future

Many people want to know what their future holds, but only God knows. Instead of worrying about the unknown, prepare yourself for paths that God may put you on.

When Christ lives in your heart and in your thoughts, you will be able to face the future without fear. Know that whatever situation and path you are confronted with, you and Christ will be able to overcome it together.

I don't know what my future holds, but I know who holds my future.

"Be strong and courageous. Do not be terrified; do not be discouraged, for the Lord your God will be with you wherever you go."
– Joshua 1:9

Who holds your future?

Seize

When you look back on your life, there may be certain highlights that tend to stand out – great moments in your life.

The truth is that every day can be one of those great moments. To experience this daily, we need to appreciate the present and the moment.

Every day is a new day, with new opportunities that God has given you.

Cherish your memories, but appreciate the importance and wonderful possibilities of today. Accept every moment of every day as a gift from God, and utilize it fully. If you do this, then every day will be a great day!!

"This is the day the Lord has made; let us rejoice and be glad in it." - Psalm 118:24

Do you seize the day?

Son

When you feel like there are dark clouds in your life, remember the 'Son' is always shining. The devil will use your dark clouds to try and hide the 'Son.'

God's love is always shining bright, but you might have to look past the dark clouds of your life to see the rays of SONshine. Trust in God and have the faith that He will carry you through the clouds.

"Remain in me, and I will remain in you."
– John 15:4

Do you see the 'Son' shining?

Wait

It can be hard to pray about our struggles because we might not be prepared for how God may answer our prayers. The answer may not be what we wanted to hear or have happen.

Remember, our God is an awesome God! He will do what is best, even if it wasn't part of our plan. Give it to God, and wait. Release your problem to Him. Think to yourself, 'God – it's your problem now, I'm done!'

Don't make suggestions; offering plan A or B. Just wait – be patient for His timing. Don't give God a deadline or a due date. Just wait and listen. Then, whatever God says – do it!

"I waited patiently for the Lord; he turned to me and heard my cry." - Psalm 40:1

Are you willing to wait?

Bridge

We have the opportunity every day to build a bridge. This bridge is between two very different worlds – those who follow Jesus and those who do not know Him.

Are you ready to build a bridge for those to cross over that do not yet know the love of God?

"Come near to God and he will come near to you." - James 4:8

Have you built a bridge?

Safety

When you are faced with temptations in life, place God between you and your temptation.

God will keep you safe and protect you from spiritual harm. He will guide you on the right path.

"I am the gate; whoever enters through me will be saved." - John 10:9

Is God your safety gate?

Will

We can get so caught up on how we want our lives to go, that sometimes our prayers become self-centered. We start to pray to God with a list of requests for our personal life.

What we need to remember to ask for when we pray, is......

"Not as I will, but as you will." – Matthew 26:39

When we pray for God's Will – we put our faith in the plan he has for our lives.

Whose will do you pray for?

Loved

You are loved more then you will ever know, by someone who died to know you.

God loves YOU! Don't push away this amazing love that you can experience in your life daily.

"Neither height nor depth, nor anything else in all creation, will be able to separate us from the love of God that is in Christ Jesus our Lord." – Romans 8:39

Do you feel loved?

ERIN LYN BURKS

Respond

Life is fragile and can change so quickly.
When this happens, how will you respond?

We can be fearful and wonder why God
allowed this to happen to us, or we can trust
that in the midst of this change He is doing
something that in the end is for our best, even
it if hurts right now.

Trust Him – His love never fails! He will hold
you in His loving arms.

"When I am afraid, I will trust in you."
– Psalm 56:3

How will you respond?

Hand

'He's Got the Whole World in His Hands.' I remember learning this song when I was little and it still relates to my life now.

Our life is in God's hands. To live our life with this belief, we must follow God's way and do His work, whatever that might be.

"My times are in your hands." – Psalm 31:15

Is your life in God's hands?

Help

It is hard to admit when we need help. It is even harder to ask for help. We need to remind ourselves to seek God's will in all we do and he will show us the path.

Ask God for help.

God will guide your footsteps, but you have to be willing to move your feet!

"My help comes from the Lord, the maker of heaven and earth." – Psalm 121:2

Do you ask for help?

Weakness

When you face problems or don't feel in-control, surrender your weaknesses in prayer to God. Ask Him to give you strength to handle each situation.

When you do this, you will be able to move forward with confidence that God's grace will enable you to overcome anything. God is by your side, He will give you strength.

"Many are the plans in a man's heart, but it is the Lord's purpose that prevails."
– Proverbs 19:21

Do you feel weak?

Prayer

God wants us to turn to Him in moments of need, but He also wants us to remember that we need Him all the time.

Prayers become a priority when we realize that we need God's help all the time. As we go through each day, don't just act on your own wisdom, but seek His will in every situation.

"Look to the Lord and his strength; seek his face always." - Psalm 105:4

Is prayer your guide or last resort?

Gift

God has given each of us many gifts in life. It is our responsibility to use the gifts we have been given.

He doesn't give us gifts simply for our own personal benefit, he wants us to use our gifts and abilities to serve and bring glory to Him.

"Each one should use whatever gift he has received to serve others, faithfully administering God's grace in its various forms." – 1 Peter 4:10

Are you using your gifts?

Patience

It is hard being patient when you lift your requests up to God. You might even feel like your prayers go unheard.

God hears and answers ALL of our prayers. BUT, we have to remember that His answers come in - His perfect timing; His perfect way; and His perfect will.

God answers our prayers according to our needs, not our wishes and will. When we pray, we need to be patient, watch & wait. When we do this, God will reveal Himself to us and show us His way in His good time.

"Devote yourselves to prayer, being watchful and thankful." – Colossians 4:2

Do you pray with patience?

Change

Life is always changing around us, but the one thing that doesn't change is God. God's word doesn't change; His promises don't change; His forgiveness of sins does not change.

God will never change!

Our moods may shift, but God's doesn't. Our mind may change, but God's doesn't. Our devotion may waver, but God's never does.

"Surely goodness and love will follow me ALL the days of my life." – Psalm 23:6

What a huge promise God has made to us – 'ALL the days of my life.' Not some, not most, but ALL …….. the days of my life!

Do you change?

Growing

It is easy to see our physical bodies grow by measuring height and weight. Our bodies can also go through spiritual growth.

Many people ignore this important aspect of growth in their lives because we can't see or measure/weigh it like our body height and weight.

The best growth advisor we can ever seek is God. We always need to seek a deeper relationship with Him.

"The mind of a sinful man is death, but the mind controlled by the Spirit is life and peace." – Romans 8:6

Are you growing spiritually?

Feed

We feed our physical bodies daily so they can function, stay healthy and active. It is just as important to make time daily to feed our spiritual bodies so they can function too, staying healthy and active in Christ.

Don't just feed your spiritual body weekly by attending church. If your spiritual body is fed daily, your whole life, body and soul, will feel great!

"I am the bread of life. He who comes to me will never go hungry, and he who believes in me will never be thirsty." – John 6:35

Did you feed your spiritual body today?

Accepted

Sometimes it can be hard to feel accepted in life. But what a wonderful gift we will receive when we get to Heaven, we will all feel accepted.

In Heaven you aren't judged or feel the pressure of society...... you are just accepted for exactly who God created you to be, YOU!

"Accept one another, then, just as Christ accepted you." - Romans 15:7

Do you feel accepted?

Searching

Throughout our life, we may find ourselves searching for something, but we also don't really know what we are searching for. We are lost.

Seek God!

Many of us seek God with only a small part of our heart....or no heart....our search is meaningless. We only seek at certain times or on certain terms. Seek God with your WHOLE heart, soul and mind.

"You will seek me and find me when you seek me with all your heart." - Jeremiah 29:13

What are you searching for?

Credit

God receives very little recognition for all the good he does in our lives. He often gets blamed when something goes wrong instead of getting credit for all the things that go right.

Every day he is watching over us. We have no idea how many times God has protected us from harm throughout our day. But when there is a tragedy, we might catch ourselves asking, 'Where was God?'

We need to remember to be thankful for all the wonderful things God does silently for us every day.

"I will exalt you and praise your name, for in perfect faithfulness you have done marvelous things." - Isaiah 25:1

Do we give God enough credit?

Predictable

We try to make our lives predictable;
organizing, planning and strategizing what we
would like to see happen in life. But then we
have to admit, this is only a guess.

We have no idea what a year, a month, a
week or even a day might bring. So we pray
and plan, and then we trust the God who
knows exactly what will happen in our lives.

"Be still, and know that I am God."
– Psalm 46:10

Life is unpredictable. But what I do know is
there is a God who knows all and loves me.
By believing in this, I can 'be still'.......I can be
at peace with the unknown.

Is your life predictable?

Listening

As a parent, I get discouraged when I try to guide my kids so they don't make a bad decision, but they won't listen.

It is hard to get them to understand that parents really do know what they are talking about. Sometimes I think, 'if they would just listen to me!'

I bet God thinks the same thing about us as our loving Father, 'if they would just listen to me!'

He has an amazing life planned out for each of us, if we would only listen to his calling.

"Speak, Lord, for your servant is listening."
– 1 Samuel 3:9

Do you listen?

Favorite

God has no 'favorites.' In God's eyes you are special because you are His child and He loves you.

Don't torture yourself trying to compare yourself to others. God made YOU to be YOU! You were created on purpose, with a purpose, for a purpose – to be YOU!

Jesus died on the cross to give salvation to all of us. He came for everyone

"For God does not show favoritism."
– Romans 2:11

Are you trying to compare to others?

Eyes

When life feels like it is dragging you down, don't put hope in the earthly things. Instead, put your hope in Heaven, eternity and God.

Open the eyes of your heart. Look with your heart and see the wonderful future that God has made possible for you, a life in heaven.

"I pray also that the eyes of your heart may be enlightened in order that you may know the hope to which he has called you, the riches of his glorious inheritance in the saints."
– Ephesians 1:18

Do you have your eyes open?

Voices

Listen....... what voice to you hear?

Do you hear God say 'I will help you' or do you hear Satan say 'God has left you?'

You get to decide which voice you listen to.

"My sheep listen to my voice; I know them, and they follow me." - John 10:27

What voice are you listening to?

Witness

It can be scary to answer God's calling, to be a witness. We can try to ignore His calling, questioning his plan for our lives. But our God can be a very persistent God. He will continue to put signs in front of you, even when you don't want to open your eyes. He will open doors that you may be scared to walk through.

There are so many ways to be a witness for God, even in just the way you lead your life.

If you are willing to witness for Him, he will be beside you every step of the way. God has equipped you with the best resource ever to be a witness - the bible.

"Now go; I will help you speak and will teach you what to say." - Exodus 4:12

Are you a witness for God?

Read

It's one thing to simply read verses from the bible, but the word of God becomes personal when you can relate it to your own life, apply it to your own life.

It is an amazing feeling when the words are popping right off the page at you. These words can give you guidance with the issues and circumstances you are dealing with.

"For this God is our God for ever and ever; he will be our guide even to the end."
– Psalm 48:14

What is God's word saying to you today?

Answers

Throughout our journey in life, our plans and God's plans may not always be the same. It is hard to admit that we don't have all the answers to life.

When you don't understand nor have the answers to why things happen to you or your loved ones, faith can help you accept and be at peace, knowing that God has all the answers.

God doesn't need to give us an explanation for His plans in our life. Trust His will-His plan.

"Trust in the Lord with all your heart and lean not on your own understanding."
– Proverbs 3:5

Do you trust God?

Perspective

Try to smile throughout the day. A smile on your face doesn't mean your life is perfect or that the day is going wonderful and as planned. It means you try to appreciate what you have and what God has blessed you with.

Happiness can come when we stop complaining about the troubles we have, and say thank you to God for the troubles we don't have.

Life is all about perspective.

"Do everything without complaining or arguing." - Philippians 2:14

Do you have perspective?

Will

Sometimes it is hard to be completely open and accepting of God's will in our life. If you start to have doubts, ask God to take control of your life and guide you on the right path.

When you ask for God's guidance, he will reveal your purpose, he will show you the path.

"Show me your ways, O Lord, teach me your paths; guide me in your truth and teach me, for you are God my Savior, and my hope is in you all day long." – Psalm 25:4-5

What is God's will for you?

Choices

Life is all about choices. If you need help making good choices, remember this simple statement:

'Do what pleases God.'

You'll never go wrong doing what is right. If we ask for guidance, God will lead us.

"For it is God who works in you to will and to act according to his good purpose."
– Philippians 2:13

What pleases God?

Necessity

Do you use God as an accessory? Praying only when you need something; asking for his guidance as a last resort when you don't feel like you can control your life?

OR

Do you use God as a necessity? Thanking him each morning for your blessings and asking for guidance upon the day ahead?

"Choose for yourself this day whom you will serve. But as for me and my household, we will serve the Lord." – Joshua 24:15

Is God an accessory or a necessity?

Mask

Sometimes a person can have inner battles that we have no idea about. Do you really know the person on the inside or just the mask they hide behind?

Some days I still feel like I am hiding behind a mask of sorrow. On the outside I try to make it look like I have it all together, but then I visit our daughter's grave and the mask comes off and the real emotions and pain show through.

Ask for God's guidance to see purpose from your pain.

"Have mercy on me, O God, have mercy on me, for in you my soul takes refuge. I will take refuge in the shadow of your wings........"
– Psalm 57:1

Do you wear a mask?

Enough

People can have a hard time knowing the difference between what they want and what they really need.

Everything we need, we can find in God. God is our provider, our healer, our comforter, our strength. God is enough.

If God is all you have, you have all you need.

"My grace is sufficient for you."
– 2 Corinthians 12:9

Is God enough for you?

Purpose

It's easy for us to feel trapped in our daily routine when we can't see a larger purpose in life. Life can start to feel dull and repetitive.

It is during days like this, remind yourself that you can serve God in every situation. Include Jesus in every aspect of your life, even your daily routine, and He will show you your purpose in life.

God will give you the vision to see your purpose.

"And we know that in all things God works for the good of those who love him, who have been called according to his purpose."
— Romans 8:28

How is your vision?

Love

It can be hard to truly comprehend just how much Jesus loves us – sinners like us.

Jesus showed us, with his arms spread wide opened, nailed to the cross. It was love, not nails that held Jesus to the cross. We are saved because of His love.

"While we were still sinners, Christ died for us." – Romans 5:8

Do you know how much Jesus loves you?

Positive

Life is all about perspective - negative vs. positive. What consumes your thoughts will consume your life

You can't think negative thoughts and expect to lead a positive life. When something negative comes into your life - challenge yourself to see how long it takes to find the positive.

You can find a positive in every situation. Sometimes it may not be easy to see, but is it always there if you look hard enough.

Life is all about perspective!

"Satisfy us in the morning with your unfailing love, that we may sing for joy and be glad all our days." - Psalm 90:14

Are you ready for the positive challenge?

Big

When we go through struggles in our life and find ourselves worrying a lot, we need to remind ourselves how big our God is.

Don't tell God how big your problem is, tell your problem how big your God is! When you have the Holy Spirit in your life, you can accomplish and overcome things you never could alone.

"For nothing is impossible with God."
– Luke 1:37

How big is your God?

Pride

Sometimes pride can get in the way of thinking we know what is best for us.

Have you ever told God, 'I'll do it my way!'

We need to remember that His way is always the best way. Humble your hearts so that you can willingly choose His way, not your way.

"I will instruct you and teach you in the way you should go; I will counsel you and watch over you." - Psalm 32:8

What way do you choose?

Priorities

Our lives always seem so busy, mostly revolving around ourselves; our families, our ambitions, our pleasures, our future, our finances. We may start to feel like life is 'all about ME.'

Do you ever wake up and say, 'What can I do for YOU today, God?'

It can sometimes be hard to put God as our main priority. MAKE time for God, don't wait to FIND time for God. Life will feel balanced when God is at the center of our life.

Try to live a more Christ-centered life rather than an I-centered life.

"He must become greater; I must become less." - John 3:30

What are your main priorities?

Fruit

Self-control – what a powerful and important fruit in our lives. A lot of damage can be done when you don't have this fruit. The secret to self-control is to be spirit-controlled.

The more we allow the Holy Spirit to direct and guide our lives, the more self-controlled our lives will become.

"But the fruit of the Spirit is love, joy, peace, patience, kindness, goodness, faithfulness, gentleness and self-control."
– Galatians 5:22-23

What kind of fruit are you looking for?

Powerful

God has blessed us with the wonderful gift of speech. He has given us the ability to use our words for encouragement, praise, witnessing and worshipping.

Our words have the power to build up, but they can also tear down if we aren't careful. Words can damage relationships, careers, ...life!

Be careful with your words, once they are said, they can only be forgiven but never forgotten

"May the words of my mouth and the meditation of my heart be pleasing in your sight." - Psalm 19:14

Do your words build up or tear down?

Double

Sometimes it is hard to remain true to our principles and not let pressures in society change us. Just because it is common doesn't mean it is right. Just because it is easy doesn't mean it is right.

Remain true to who you really are, feel blessed with the joy of knowing that you aren't living a double life.

Strive to please God rather than society. When you are at peace with yourself, you will be able to live a life of quality and contentment.

"Do not conform any longer to the pattern of the world, but be transformed by the renewing of your mind." – Romans 12:2

Are you leading a double life?

Obstacles

Life is full of obstacles. When we experience these trials, we can either make excuses or find solutions.

If it isn't important and not a priority, we will make excuses, finding barriers and obstacles.

If something is important enough to us we will search for a solution and find a way. If it matters, we will find the time, make the time.

"I can do everything through him who gives me strength." – Philippians 4:13

Do you look for solutions or make excuses?

Friendship

Friendship is about quality not quantity. Your circle of friends may decrease in size, but increase in value.

Positive friends help you find a way to rise up. They motivate; inspire; and celebrate YOU!

True friends know when to say something, and when to just listen. Friends are God's way of taking care of us.

"A friend loves at all time." – Proverbs 17:17

What type of friends do you have?

Alone

If you feel that you have no one to turn to for help and comfort in times of trouble, remember that God is always with you.

You are never alone in this world – God is always by your side.

Turn to Him and remember that he will never leave you nor forsake you.

"I am with you always, to the very end of the age." – Matthew 28:20

Do you turn to God?

Joy

Who remembers singing, 'I've got the joy, joy, joy, joy, down in my heart' as a child? Life is all about perspective and how we react to events that happen in our life. If we look hard enough, we can always find a positive in every situation.

Don't let anyone or anything take your joy! Next time you are tempted to become upset, frustrated, or offended, remind yourself there will always be circumstances in life that you can't control. However, you can control how you respond.

Say to yourself, 'you can't take my joy!' When you make this statement, you will feel powerful and victorious, like you have won the battle, because your joy wasn't taken.

"....and no one will take away your joy."
- John 16:22

Do you have joy in your heart?

What-if

'What' & 'If' are two very non threatening words, but put them together, side-by-side and they can cause very powerful thoughts - 'What if?'

Don't let the what-ifs of life consume your thoughts. It is disappointing to God when we show that we don't have faith and trust Him to always be with us, to guide us, to protect us, to lead us.

"Do not be anxious about anything, but in everything, by prayer and petition, with thanksgiving, present your requests to God."
- Philippians 4:6

What if?

Peace

It is a lot easier to enjoy life when you live in peace and harmony. We can all experience this type of life, if we can find peace within ourselves.

When circumstances try to get the better of you, think 'peace be with you.' If you are fighting with others or holding on to hurtful thoughts, think 'peace be with you.'

"Peace I leave with you; my peace I give you."
- John 14:27

Do you have peace?

Content

Contentment comes from looking at God, resentment comes from looking at others. If you find yourself not feeling content with life, remind yourself that God has not short-changed you. He has already given you everything you need to accomplish the work He wants you to do.

When God assigns work, he also provides resources. Our only assignment is to use whatever time and talents he has given us in a way that blesses others and gives God the glory.

"For we are God's workmanship, created in Christ Jesus to do good works, which God prepared in advance for us to do."
– Ephesians 2:10

Did you complete your assignment?

Timing

Sometimes it is hard to accept God's perfect timing instead of our own planned timing. During those difficult stages in life, we have to increase our faith and remind ourselves that God's timing is always perfect, even though it may not seem that way at the moment.

When HIS WILL becomes our primary concern, then we can start to understand God's perfect timing. We only see the current picture of our lives, but God sees the greater picture of our entire life.

"I am the Lord; in its time I will do this swiftly."
– Isaiah 60:22

Do you see God's perfect timing?

Comfort

The troubles and pressures of life can drive us to seek comfort in different things; chocolate, food, alcohol ...... The best way to handle the problems and tensions of life is by having faith in Christ.

Come to Him in all circumstances, talk to Him, hold on to Him. Regardless of how desperate your situation might be, trust in Him. Trust that He is always with you.

His peace will fill your heart and help you overcome all your fears.

"In this world you will have trouble. But take heart! I have overcome the world."
– John 16:33

How do you find comfort?

One-way

Do you have a one-way prayer life with God, only telling God what you need?

Prayer should be a two-way process. You tell God what you want from Him and He reveals to you what He expects from you. Ensure you listen to God in prayer as much as you want Him to listen to your prayers.

"In the morning, O Lord, you hear my voice; in the morning I lay my requests before you and wait in expectation." - Psalm 5:3

Are you living life on a one-way street?

Bumps

The path of life that we are traveling on can sometimes feel real bumpy. We may start to question, 'Am I on the wrong path, so God made it bumpy?' or do you ask, 'Am I on the right path that God has planned for me, but he purposefully made the road bumpy to test me?'

Just because we are on the path of life that God chose for us, doesn't mean it will be easy. God doesn't promise a smooth path, but He promises to hold our hand as we walk on this bumpy path together.

Pray for God's guidance to know which path you should be on.

"The Lord will guide you always."
– Isaiah 58:11

Are you on the right path?

By God

Have you ever heard someone say, 'by God!' when they want to make a statement? We need to remind ourselves daily that we need God's help and guidance in our lives.

Instead of saying, 'by God!' when we want to make a statement, say, 'by God's way!'

"As for God, his way is perfect; the word of the Lord is flawless." - Psalm 18:30

Whose way?

Life

While we can't always control the things of life that effect our day, we do have a choice. We can continue to get upset over those things or we can change our perspective.

Pray for God to bless you with the wisdom to change your perspective rather then let life change you. Pray for wisdom to see things from God's perspective.

Life is all about perspective

"In his heart a man plans his course, but the Lord determines his steps." - Proverbs 16:9

Do you need to change perspective?

Grace

It is important to some people to be recognized for everything they do. However, our works don't earn us salvation, Jesus already earned that for us.

We need to want to work for a cause, not for praise. Live life to express our gratitude to God, not to impress others. Try not to make your presence noticed, but have your absence sensed.

"For it is by grace you have been saved, through faith – and this not from yourselves, it is the gift of God – not by works, so that no one can boast." – Ephesians 2:8-9

Got grace?

Gift

Do you truly appreciate God's gifts? Do you think they are good enough or do you find yourself thinking that He could have done better?

Sadly, sometimes we have limited understanding and don't realize the prepared blessing God is still working on in our life.

We need to be patient and wait for His time, not our time. We need to trust that the Lord who loves us enough to save us will always, ALWAYS do what is best for us.

"Every good and perfect gift is from above, coming down from the Father of the heavenly lights." - James 1:17

What gift did God give you today?

Journey

God has a journey planned for each of us. The journey to our eternal home may be a short walk of just 25 days like our infant daughter Ashley; or an extended trip of 100+ years and still going, as my grandma continues on her journey.

No matter if our walk is measured in days or years; cherish each step you are blessed with. We are all on the journey of life, walking towards our eternal home in heaven. None of us know when we will celebrate our eternal homecoming or how long our walk will be. Only God knows.

We must embrace this wonderful life we have been blessed with, every second, every moment, every day is a gift- cherish it!

"All the days ordained for me were written in your book before one of them came to be."
- Psalm 139:16

Do you cherish your steps?

MEET THE AUTHOR

I have been happily married to the love of my life and best friend for 17 years. We are blessed to be raising two amazing sons; Jacob is 13 and Caleb is 11.

We feel fortunate to raise our family in a wonderful rural community. We enjoy outdoor activities, DIY projects and volunteering in our church & community.

God blessed me with a calling upon my heart to write 'Every day is a gift.' As I celebrate life and go through trials, I have discovered I can handle anything when I ensure God is at the center of my life.

"I can do everything through him who gives me strength."
– Philippians 4:13

Making time for daily devotions helps keep God at the core of my life and reminds me to seek Him in everything that I do.

I pray that 'Every day is a gift' daily devotions will help keep God at the center of your life too.

52687363R00061

Made in the USA
Charleston, SC
23 February 2016